DEVELOPING A
SPIRITUAL
PARTNERSHIP

DEVELOPING A SPIRITUAL PARTNERSHIP

BRINGING SPIRITUALITY
INTO YOUR
RELATIONSHIP
BEFORE, DURING, AND AFTER
THE "I DO'S"

CHARLANN WALKER
INTERFAITH MINISTER

ILLUSTRATED BY

SUSAN KIBBE-ALLAIRE

Library of Congress Number:		2005902299
ISBN :	Hardcover	1-4134-9010-7
	Softcover	1-4134-9009-3

This book was printed in the United States of America.

To order additional copies of this book, contact:
Xlibris Corporation
1-888-795-4274
www.Xlibris.com
Orders@Xlibris.com
27558

Contents

*This book is dedicated to my
daughter Jennifer and my son Jacob.
And for all those who live and love in ritual.*

Ancient Sufi Prayer

I offer you peace.
I offer you joy.
I offer you friendship.

I hear your needs.
I see your beauty.

Our wisdom comes from
a Higher Source.
Our wisdom comes from
a deeper source.
I honor that Source in you.

Preface

Congratulations. You have picked up this book because you sense a deep desire within to bring spirituality into your lives, before, during, and after the wedding ceremony. There is so much hoopla before the wedding ceremony that it is important to provide a time-out during certain intervals. This book is the result of many years of working with couples in developing unique wedding services that are spiritually and personally meaningful.

Within the first part of this book are ideas for those special interludes including a collection of different kinds of spiritually based rituals, uses for aromatherapy, special relaxation methods, meditations, treasure mapping, and more.

In the second section are special suggestions for bringing spirituality within the wedding ceremony: ideas and suggestions about writing your own vows, choosing special readings, and inserting different symbolism within the context of the ceremony. There are many ways to fashion your service in order to express your love for each other, such as the Stone Blessing, Flower Ceremony, Handfasting, Water Ceremony, and the list goes on.

The third section deals with spiritual suggestions and ideas to work with after the "I do's." In building your life together, you may want to consider including family meetings, providing time to journal together, or even planting a tree in honor of your relationship.

Sharing and Planning

Marriage is one of the most serious and important steps that most of us enter into. The marriage ceremony announces the beginning of a new life. It sets the stage for a chance at fulfilling long-held dreams and opportunities for great personal and spiritual growth.

More now then ever, couples search for different ways to bring a new dimension into their wedding ceremony and into their lives together. They want words and ritual to create a personalized ceremony that others will call "blessed." They want a ceremony that will be remembered by all as sacred.

Much effort goes into the planning of a wedding, be it large or small. There are so many details and uncertainties that may occur. Today, many couples reject the textbook wedding and opt to hold their ceremonies in nontraditional ways. Couples are stretching the rules. They want to change the format of the past and consider other options. Celebrating a union in a country club, on the beach, or under an outdoor canopy at a yacht club is becoming the norm. Others honor their joining standing by a fire in a mansion or even out on the water on a sailing vessel.

Sometimes couples infuse personal styles and customs including different religious sentiments or ceremonial seasonal reflections. A Judeo-Christian couple wanted to incorporate a flavor of their different religious backgrounds, along with the strong feeling of family. They combined their privately written vows, the presentation of roses to parents that is drawn from the Catholic tradition, the breaking of a wine glass that is traditional in the Jewish ceremony, and the lighting of the family unity candle. One could also choose to include the traditional garland exchange, which is part of the Hindu ceremony.

In today's weddings, many rules disappear. The mainstream dissolves, and in its place, we find the birthing of a new nuptial icon. We feel pulled toward what is living in all traditions and then incorporate each facet in a pleasing and inspirational service. Weddings are now a mix of the traditional, alternative, mystical, and spiritual.

Many couples desire to incorporate the old with the new, the traditional with the nontraditional, and weave it all into a wedding ceremony that spells "unique." The question is how to design a ceremony that reflects the belief that your marriage is a profound expression of your relationship, yet does not make you feel as if it came from a catalog.

The answer is in the joint planning, the common sharing, and, most importantly, by providing an openness to allow spirit to flow through. By doing this, couples can honor the sacredness and the uniqueness of each other as a pair, as well as individually, thus creating a path where both can meet on common ground. Couples contribute to the whole while fulfilling their own unique roll. Then, with this spirit of openness, one can discover new ways to worship and to participate in ritualistic and meaningful ceremonies of life.

What Is Spirituality?

Life is an adventure, and every day we encounter signs that lead the way to the presence of a Creator, a Spirit, or a Universal One that surrounds us and calls upon us.

We look in the woods, we look to the sky, we sit in silence, we meditate, and this is called spirituality. Getting in touch with our source, or our center, is at the core of spirituality.

For me, my quiet times are near a pond located in my backyard where I meditate upon things in life that are important to me at a given time. Water plays a strong part in my life, and I find I am nearer to my source when I am near the water.

Where is your special place that gives you peace and serenity and where you can carve spirituality into your life? Do you like the mountains? Do you like to hike or just walk in the woods? Do you prefer working in the woods, or just sitting peacefully in your lounge chair?

Wherever one can create a place of restfulness needed to sustain us, that special place is called the center of spirituality.

Most couples, even though they may choose not to attend a church or a temple, do possess a deep sense of spirituality and wish to include it in their ceremony and in their life together.

It is good to lift our spiritual life in order to boost the soul and enrich the spirit. Doing this on a regular basis is special. Perhaps this can be done with readings, with meditation, and especially by planning ahead to include some sort of commitment to spirituality in the years following the wedding ceremony.

In the dew of little things
the heart finds its meaning
and is refreshed.

—Kahlil Gibran

Rituals to Create a Time-Out

After the Announcement

You lived through the excitement of the announcement. Now you are settling into the throes of the planning. This is a thrilling time, but let's face it; maybe you are on a short-time schedule, or maybe your families are coming in from all different directions creating more decisions to be made. Whatever the issues, stress is felt.

The question is how do you make your times alone special? You could read poetry, try a crossword puzzle together, or just talk about things that really count to both of you.

Instead of saying, "I don't have the time," ask yourself, "How can I bring spirituality into my life now?" It is true that your responsibilities are overwhelming. But it is also true that quiet time is most important. Quiet time brings one closer to the source within and to one another.

Rather than creating our days in the form of a fast-paced circle of "stuff to be done," it is helpful to frame life's passages in the form of ritual.

Rituals can honor all the phases in our life. Life is a series of passages, which connect us to each other. They link us to the seasons and lead us through our paths in life. Each passage provides us with a fresh new opportunity to mark our changes and to make celebrations. This means allowing for exclusive time and exclusive space, where there are absolutely no interruptions or distractions.

Rituals bring our attention inward. They transform us by taking the ordinary into the sacred. They can be held privately or in a group. It is good to bless where we are in life, who we are, and how we live with words, symbols, images, sounds, colors, movements, and smells. This can help us focus on the fact that there is much more to our lives than the apparent current state of choices and questions that may plague us to distraction.

Now is a perfect time to take a time-out and reflect with silence and ritual on your new status. Honor the places in your life, and this honoring will reflect back to you.

Now is the time to stop and to bring ritual into your lives. Breathe in, and then participate in the simple act of welcoming where you are in this time and in this place.

I wish the days to be as centuries, loaded, fragrant.
—Ralph Waldo Emerson, *Considerations by the Way*

Try Just Breathing

When you are in the flurry of the moment and unable to make a decision, then just breathe. Sit in some comfortable seats. One of you may read the following passage. Then both of you take about ten minutes in silence to reflect on what you have heard and read.

Recognize yourselves as the unique individuals you are. Appreciate who you are, where you have come from, and where you are going. After your ten minutes or so of silence, you may wish to discuss what happened in your quiet time. Many ideas may have come up in this time, and it is good to explore with each other your ideas and your thoughts. After this, you may want to take that walk in the woods.

The task is to breathe and to be mindful of the spirit and of the breath of life.

Within the center of your body, the chapel of your body, in the blood and bone and star stuff of your body, moves the spirit of who you were.

Recognize yourself as that person of your youth: hopeful, beautiful, wild, wide-eyed, wide open to the world, unencumbered as your spirit moves in to embrace you.

Within the center of your body moves the spirit of who you are now. Recognize yourself as the creator of your life, the maker of things that have happened to you, both good and good for learning. You are the person who is growing within, and you accept yourself just as you are.

Within the center of your body resides the future of you. Recognize yourself and welcome the incoming you as you unfold and continue to develop—fearless, knowing, listening, and loving your life. Your wisdom, intuition, and ancient instinct are the things you know without being told, the things you've learned by being you.

What Is Faith?

Now is the time when you will be meeting with the person you have chosen to officiate your wedding ceremony. If you are affiliated with a local church or a temple, then that person already knows you and what your beliefs may be. If you need to look for an officiant, then that person may start asking you questions about your faith.

Faith is a belief in things that your senses may not have yet experienced and you do not understand, but has touched you in a way that is unfathomable. It is an unshakable belief in the presence of a god, or a creator, or in some great source beyond oneself.

But faith does not necessarily pertain only to your religious beliefs. One can have faith in family, in relationships. Some mentor may have instilled great faith in you because they helped you through a terrible crisis.

For me, I have faith in the power of prayer, and I believe that by praying, a healing will occur in mind, body, and soul. My prayers are affirmative prayers that encourage me to rethink and rephrase what needs to be changed in my life. Instead of looking at life through clouded glasses, my prayers recharge me with a positive effect of knowing all will be well, no matter the outcome.

An interfaith understanding is important now because it unites differences between various religions and philosophies. It does not divide. Instead it can enrich our lives and deepen our spirituality.

Taking time out to discuss your belief systems now is healthy because it paves the way for ideas to be included in your ceremony, as well as shoring up a strong foundation in your marriage. And then in the end, you may choose to have your ceremony reflect different traditions and religions. In your discussions, consider recording some of these ideas and feelings. Here are some questions you can start asking each:

- What religious beliefs have you had through your life and how have they changed or developed?

- What person or group stretched your spiritual beliefs and imagination?

- Have you experienced a major crisis in your life and how has that impacted on your faith?

- How can we combine our beliefs so that we can challenge each of us to greater heights?

> *If one advances confidently in the direction of his dreams, and endeavors to live the life which he has imagined, he will meet with a success unexpected in common hours.*
>
> —Thoreau

Special Touchstones

Many of us use different devotional tools to live in a state of mindfulness. Mindfulness means simply to think about what you are doing in that moment. Not to have your thoughts jump in the past or in the future. One of the ways I bring my mind to a mindfulness state is to collect all sorts of stones and pebbles and rocks at the beach. Then I set them up in my garden so I may look at them and remember the moments I found them. I search for rocks in order to foster patience, to reach clarity, to live in gratitude. When I touch them, their smoothness brings me calm. When I look at them, I feel closer to nature. I like round ones, flat ones, and heart shaped. I like big ones, black ones, and white ones. I like them all.

I like to place them in my house. I have quartz crystals, fluorites, amethysts, and pieces of petrified wood. I have small touching stones in my bag that I hold when I need to be reminded to go within and to still my soul. I carry stones in my pockets, which include a favorite stone from Hawaii's volcanoes and a rose quartz.

What are your favorite touchstones? They do not need to be stones but could be other tools that will bring you to your center. Decide what they are, and take your partner to the beach, to the woods, wherever, and together search for your favorite free things in life. Take a few hours out of your busy time and find yourself that special token.

You can bring home your treasures and find a special way to place them. They could be placed on a tray, on a table, or even in a shadow box that you have created together.

A couple built a square box about the size of two by two feet and lined it with copper. The front side was open, and they found items to include in their shadow box. There was a soapstone statue of a woman kneeling, a small rectangular mirror hung on the back wall of the box, some shells on the floor of the box, and a little table with a tiny vase and dried flowers sat to one side. When it was finished, they placed it on their fireplace mantle facing outward. The point is they did it together. They continue to add items and move things around. It is lovely and certainly a piece that calls one's attention. Now is the time for you to create opportunities to, again, remember your day in nature.

> *Take your cares to Mother Earth*
> *and the great healing spirit of nature.*
>
> —Anonymous

Art of Meditation

Meditation is a wonderful way to bring spirituality into your lives. There are many ways to meditate. You can meditate with a favorite stone that you have picked up from the beach. Or you may have other devotional tools you wish to use: beads, crosses, or trinkets.

> *The first thing*
> *The last thing.*
> *Start from where you are.*
> —Dale Pendell

Here is another way you can both meditate together. First, light candles and get comfortable. One of you may read the following readings, and then you can both go into silence for a few minutes. Set a timer for five minutes. After the timer rings, you may want to share some of your feelings or any epiphanies that may have sparked your attention.

Maybe in your travels you will find more random collections of thoughts, words, and phrases that you may want to mediate with. Save them in a book or journal to be used at a later date. I know that many find it difficult to meditate alone, let alone with a partner. But the trick is to try it and see what happens. You may be surprised. Be patient with yourself.

Be still
Listen to the stones of the wall.
Be silent, then try
to speak your
name.
Listen
to the living walls
Who are you?
Who
Are you? Whose
Silence are you.

—Thomas Merton

Live in joy
In love,
Even among those who hate.
Live in joy,
in health,
even among the afflicted.
Live in joy,
in peace
even among the troubled.
Live in joy,
Without possessions
Like the shining ones.

—*The Dhammapada:*
Sayings of the Buddha

Treasure Mapping

Many experts in the field of metaphysics and psychotherapy tell us that our thoughts and creative ideas help form the world we live in. Our thoughts help shape the course of our lives. These same experts suggest that individuals use the practice of creative imagery. This is a deep relaxation method, which allows us to harness our imagination to make positive changes in our lives.

The project I am suggesting to use creative imagery with is called "treasure mapping." This method uses all the senses, not just the ability to visualize. So whatever may be lacking in your life, or if you have decisions to be made, this is a good way to project their possibility into reality.

To begin with, collect your favorite magazines and your colored pens and other supplementary writing materials. Set the room up with candles or perhaps scent the space with such essential oils as ylang ylang or fragrance oils such as tea rose. These special scents lull you to a place of peace and romance.

Plump up some pillows or seat yourself in that special comfortable chair and start flicking through the magazines. (I like to spread everything out on the floor.) Then select pictures that appeal to you. You may want to have a theme in mind before you start cutting the pictures or words that appeal to you. Your theme may be any of the following:

- Where do I want to live?

- What will the inside of my house look like?

- How do I want to improve my physical health?

- A reverie of landscapes—beautiful pictures

Try and select a topic that promises new opportunities or one that revolves around friendships, security, or abundance. Have fun with these ideas. After selecting a subject, start cutting the appropriate photos, which fills your requirements. You may want to purchase a large colored poster board for mounting the pictures. Don't forget the glue.

When you have collected all the photos that resonate, then you are ready to create a collage of the cuttings. Simply paste them in a meaningful way. You may want to consider the artistic rendition that you have chosen.

This could take a couple of hours, and when you are ready, you can mount the finished piece on a wall as a reminder of your intentions, or tuck it away so that only you can see it. You can add to it at a later time if you wish, or you can make an entire new one with another theme.

This is a powerful form of creative imagery, and the process is enjoyable and relaxing. It is fun to do it together. This project focuses the mind on the desires and makes them the dominant thoughts rather than any stresses which may be present in your life.

I create new treasure maps all the time. As a matter of fact, I feel like doing another right now, and maybe I will center it on a healthy and a pretty appearance. You think this is too vain? Well, why not? When we feel good about ourselves, we do feel closer to the source within and attract experiences that affirm our new way of thinking.

Create Harmony in
Heart and Home

Incense is an important tool to help calm the senses, still the mind, and create an atmosphere to become mindful in the moment. Scents have the ability to change a mood, make an experience more vivid, intense or powerful, as well as create a more pleasing environment.

I light incense all the time and experiment with different fragrances for different moments. There are so many different kinds of incense, as well as fragrances, but right here, I just want to talk about some ways to incorporate the use of incense into your life.

There are several ways couples can use incense. Don't forget to use incense in some of the other rituals mentioned within these pages.

Smudging

In many religious and spiritual traditions, individuals practice the burning of herbs for emotional, psychic, and spiritual purification. In the American Indian traditions, using a smudge stick was a way for them to cleanse a person, place, or an object of negative energies, spirits, or influences. Smudging is good when you may feel depressed, angry, or resentful.

You may want to smudge when you have had an argument with someone. In Native American societies, the herbs used for smudging are considered sacred.

A smudge stick is made by wrapping different herbs such as cedar, sage and/or lavender. You can purchase smudge sticks from the same places you obtain your incense or, of course, go on line.

I find that it is particularly centering to have an intention in mind when doing this. One intention can be when you are renting, buying, or selling your home or apartment. This is an excellent time to use a smudge stick. In smudging your room or house before you leave it, you may want to affirm that your dwelling place is a temple for body or spirit.

Purifying your house before you sell it is so beneficial. It acts as an opportunity for sharing gratitude and thanks, as well as a release. For the ceremony, you may want to invite some friends, have a light evening dinner, and afterward develop an agenda for the blessing and release. After you announce what you are doing, you may want to go from room to room with incense or a smudge stick. Or you may want to perform this ceremony alone.

Two souls with but a single thought.
Two hearts that beat as one.
—Friedrich Hahn

If you are buying a house, you may want to do the same thing. Invite friends, have dinner, and then smudge the home. Hold the smudge stick in a clay bowl or abalone shell to catch the ashes. Go to each room, making sure the scent enters all the four corners of each room. Ask for blessings, prosperity, and health of the home and for all the people who live there and who visit as caring visitors.

More about Incense and Quiet

Silence and Spaciousness
go together.
—J. Krishnamurti

Burning incense has the power to transform us by doing it in quiet way. If you have a fireplace, pop a cone incense on your fire in the hearth while you enjoy a quiet moment. If not, simply light a cone in a shell or dish. Each of you may want to pick up a journal and start writing your thoughts to the smell of jasmine. Here are some benefits of incense stated by Ikkyu, a priest of the Rinzai sect of Buddhism in the Muromachi Era:

Incense brings communication with the transcendent.

It cleanses and purifies the mind and body.

It brings alertness.

It is a companion to solitude.

In the midst of activity, it brings a moment of peace.

Used every day, it does no harm.

It can be used in small or large quantities.

Tea Time

Here are some words about tea and tea for two. Now, now, don't laugh. I know some of you may not enjoy tea, but now is your chance to experiment.

There are many types of tea, and it is fun to experiment with different tastes. You can get lost in the subject of tea and its complexities. It takes time, but for me, tea is a solace, a companion. It is a cool drink in the summer and a cozy drink by the fire when it snows. Lately, green tea seems to suit my fancy. I like to steep the loose leaves in a pot and watch as I pour it into a lovely cup that I picked up at a local antique shop. I found the cup tucked away behind some other plates and bowls. I plucked it out, wiped off the dust, and brought it home for a pittance.

But tea is not only for pleasure. Tea contains many healthy benefits. Scientists, around the world, have researched and examined the tea leaf and feel they know the answers as to why this simple beverage is so important.

Tea is good for oral health and provides benefits for teeth and bones. The vital chemical compounds that make up the tea leaf have been found to help fight cancer, help stabilize diabetes, and do much to prevent cardiovascular disease. Taken on a regular basis, it is even good for your skin.

So have fun experimenting with the different teas. Don't stop with black teas, but try some oolong, Lapsang Souchong, jasmine, white tea, Rooibos . . . and the list goes on.

Dried Herbs

Herbal teas awaken healing properties and the mere act of making teas act as a remedy in itself. According to the *Women's Book of Healing*, there are many herbal tea blends to help with different physical complaints. Here are a couple of herb teas you can use for anxiety. Of course, check with your doctor if you are nursing or pregnant.

You can try valerian, skullcap, passionflower, or chamomile. I like to put about two teaspoons of the herbs I am using in a pot of boiling water. Let it steep for a while, pour and enjoy.

For a quick calm-down formula, try one ounce of Siberian ginseng, licorice root, and skullcap and one-half ounce each of marshmallow and valerian. This may be helpful in strengthening the adrenal glands as well as soothing and nourishing the nerves. I like to mix spearmint leaves with nettles and lemon balm for a pick-me-up.

Of course, you have to find a good dried herb shop that sells these herbs, or else go on line to locate a direct mail order company that specializes in organic dried herbs. But most communities have a health food store, which can supply you with the basics.

Tea for This Couple

Here is a way to use a cup of tea as a way of recalling that first time when you looked at each other and began this journey.

One couple whom I recently married are both chiropractors and are just setting up their business after having graduated from school. They both learned many different ways of relaxing, but the one they found the most comfortable was to start out with a short walk around their favorite woodsy spot. They talk about their dreams, their hopes, and their wishes.

When they come home, they have a gourmet platter waiting for them. They enjoy a cup of tea and munch on their special treats. They drink it slowly and with pleasure. As they munch and drink, they do it in silence and spend at least one-half hour in this restful state. This is a planned time and a planned activity. It does not need to take up an entire day.

Walking in Mindfulness

Talking about walking, what a wonderful way to get out, breathe fresh air, and be together. Walking in mindfulness gathers the senses and creates peace and calm. Walking in mindfulness means to be present in every moment. Paying attention to each step taken is the act of mindfulness. Walking in nature and in quiet can provide amazing insights.

Vietnamese Zen Master Thich Nhat Hanh writes, "People say that walking on water is a miracle, but to me walking peacefully on Earth is the real miracle. The Earth is a miracle. Taking steps on our beautiful planet brings real happiness and peace to ourselves and our world."

But walking in silence is hard especially when you may want to share ideas, projects, and things that are happening. You want to talk and to share. Thich Nhat Hanh says that images make the practice easy, and the following poetry is one of the images he uses for walking meditation. Think about the following words and the images while holding hands and being together. Start to focus on your body movements at the same time with your breaths. Feel your footsteps on the ground as you walk along. Feel the air enter your lungs. Focus on as much of your body as you can until it becomes natural. When you find your mind wandering, go back and think about the words.

Breathing in, I know I am breathing in.

Breathing out, I know I am breathing out.

(*Breathe in and then out.*)

Breathing in, I see myself as a flower.

Breathing out, I feel fresh.

(*Visualize being as fresh as a flower.*)

Breathing in, I am solid as a mountain.

Breathing out, I am firm as the earth.

(*Visualize being solid as a mountain.*)

Breathing in, I see myself as still water.

Breathing out, I reflect things as they are.

(*Visualize the water reflecting.*)

Breathing in, I see myself as space.

Breathing out, I feel free.

(*Visualize space and free.*)

When you are finished walking, you will find a greater peace. This will help both of you concentrate on the issues with a clearer mind. This helps to quiet the mind in order to hear what the spirit has to reveal. Before you share your experience over a cup of jasmine tea, here are some guidelines to establish beforehand. These guidelines will help you in your role together as a couple.

- Promise each other that you will both be good listeners.

- Promise each other that you will provide a safe environment so that both of you will feel comfortable enough to share your deeper thoughts.

- Promise each other that there will be no judging of feelings or ideas.

By acting on these promises, your spiritual journey together will be peaceful and the goodness will shine through.

Sharing Feelings

This is a very exciting time in your lives. In the next few months before your wedding, you will spend time not only gathering information and planning for the actual day but also thinking about your future lives together. Here are some questions you may want to ask yourself in planning your life as a couple. The answers to these questions can be used in different ways. You may want to use some of your thoughts as part of your vows for your wedding ceremony. You may want to include some of your feelings in other parts of your ceremony.

Before you start, it might be nice to prepare the room by lighting some candles or incense, have some paper and pencil ready, have some refreshments on the table. As Antoine de Saint-Exupery wrote, "Love is not looking into one another's eyes, but looking together in the same direction." Keep those words within your heart while you explore your feelings. Most importantly, this is not a time for judgment or criticism. It is time for sharing and exploration.

Questions

- What is it that each of us most appreciates in the other?

- For us, what are the most important things in the world?

- What are our core values?

- What is the most special thing about our relationship?

- What would we like to be able to say about our relationship as we look back on it, say in forty years time?

- Why are we getting married?

Bringing Spirituality in Your Wedding Ceremony

Your Wedding

It is a different world today, and many couples now enjoy a new kind of freedom in planning their marriage ceremony and deciding on its location. Many couples opt to hold their weddings in country clubs, mansions, state parks, and backyards. Many couples choose to follow different traditions, as well as unusual ways of celebrating.

Together, you can design an unforgettable ceremony that will be memorable and written expressly for you. It will be joyous, personal, solemn, and spiritually meaningful. The most important ingredients in the wedding ceremony include sharing, spirituality, and graciousness.

The earth laughs in flowers;
A flower is love looking for a word.

If you are getting married in a destination wedding, you will need to find a minister who will agree to officiate as well as travel to your location. Following are some questions to ask the minister whom you are thinking of hiring. This will help in the decision making.

Is this person flexible enough to include various readings or other rituals that may reflect who you are as a couple?

Perhaps you may want to have a destination wedding and hold it in a garden, hotel, inn, yacht, private club, or a private home. Are they willing to travel to special locations?

Do you want to write your own vows? Will the officiant work with you on this?

What does the officiant wear?

Do they provide their own sound equipment?

Do they attend rehearsals?

Are they flexible enough to make changes?

Do they schedule too many weddings back-to-back? This is a no-no.

Do you feel comfortable and have a connection with the officiant?

Planning Your Wedding

In the book *The Language of the Brides* are written some wonderful quotes from different couples and individuals that give unique insights about their weddings and their togetherness. I found them profound and helpful. Here are their simple words of wisdom taken from the book:

From Cokie and Steve Roberts,

> *The whole process, painful as it was at times, taught us a great deal about solving problems, showing patience, focusing on what was truly important. And looking back, it's clear the wedding became a metaphor for how we would live our lives together.*

From Jane Andrews,

> *Don't let the planning of your wedding overshadow the ultimate goal—the important thing is that you get to spend the rest of your life with the one you love. And though the process may test your relationship at times, working toward that moment when you get to say "I do" should be a time to strengthen your love.*

From Emily Chase,

> *We have looked back to the days before our wedding many times. It's often been a source of*

strength for us to know that we could plan something so important together and have the outcome be a true expression of our love. Because we each made a conscious effort to share the planning tasks as equally as possible, our wedding day and vows meant so much to both of us and we've never forgotten their importance.

From anonymous,

We made a decision early on in the planning of our wedding that no matter what happened, no matter what went wrong, or what was less than perfect, no matter who messed up their entrances or their lines, or who was late or didn't show up at all, we were going to laugh about it and enjoy ourselves. And that is exactly what we did. Our day couldn't have been more perfect. It went off without a hitch. This is your day! You have been looking forward to it all your life! Enjoy it. Let nothing hinder it. Have fun with it all and don't worry about details. Think about waking up every day next to the person you love most.

Order of Service

The following are two examples of the ways couples may elect to have the order of their service. There are many different ways and rituals to include as you will find in the coming pages of this book. It is fun to play around with your ideas and the meaning behind the different ways. A good suggestion is to construct the ceremony to last about twenty-five to thirty minutes.

Sample 1:

> Music
> Invocation and Candle Lighting
> Welcome
> Foundation
> Reading
> Ring Ceremony
> Reading
> Unity Candle Lighting
> Minister's Blessing
> The Charge
> Pronouncement
> Music

Sample 2:

Music
Welcome
Minister's Introduction
First Reading
Wine Ceremony
Second Reading
Ring Ceremony
The Blessing
Pronouncement
Music

All about Vows . . .

Vows are considered the part of the wedding, which is the Statement of Intent. These words may make up a lifelong promise to one another and should not be taken lightly.

Bookshops are filled with books containing ideas for the wedding ceremony. Vows are important for your wedding ceremony, and you may find different ways to present them.

You may want to write your own. Finding the right words may bit a bit challenging, but you may find appropriate words in prose or poetry or other sources that inspire both of you. One of the things you may want to ask each other is, "What promises do you wish to fulfill in this marriage?"

You may decide to say the traditional vows: "I take thee . . ." And some couples may add their personal feelings to the traditional words.

You may ask the officiant to write them, and if they are amenable, this may be an option. Sometimes I write vows for couples after I find out about their relationship and how they feel about one another. Then they have the option of reviewing what I write and are able to make changes.

One couple I married exchanged numerous love letters throughout their relationship. Each decided to pick one from their stack and use this as part of their vows. They printed it on parchment paper, rolled it like a scroll, and tied it with colorful ribbon. It contained all the important ingredients of good vows—their love for each other, that their love will be sustained, and that they will honor each other forever.

Personally, I do not recommend memorizing them. In the rush of the day, words may be hard to remember, and it can be made even more distracting.

In the book *Wedding Vows*, Michael Macfarlane discusses how vows can fit wedding venues. While I do not believe in having weddings in really obscure locations, I do like to officiate weddings which are held in special sites that are tastefully selected.

> *My bounty is as boundless as the sea,*
> *My love as deep:*
> *the more I give thee,*
> *the more I have,*
> *for both are infinite.*
> —William Shakespeare, *Romeo and Juliet*

Readings

On the following pages are a few examples of readings that couples may choose to consider reading during the ceremony. Those selected here reflect the more unusual ones. When you pick someone to read—a friend or a relative—first, make sure they want to do this honored gesture; and next, make sure they are able do it. It is difficult even with a microphone to hear a soft or muffled voice.

When selecting readings, ask the minister or priest if you can make suggestions. Many prefer scripture readings from the Bible or other holy books. Other ministers allow more freedom in helping to suggest appropriate readings. Take care in making your selections. The words spoken at your wedding must be as profound and powerful, as are the other parts of your ceremony.

In the book *Sacred Threshold*, Gertrud Mueller Nelson and Christopher Witt talk about the importance of taking care in making a reading selection. They break it up into categories to be considered:

1. Be sure to choose something that all the people you have gathered at your wedding are capable of understanding.

2. You may want your reading to draw from the

shared heritage of the community you have gathered to witness your wedding.

3. Give your guests something profound in your selected reading. Avoid the lightweight, frivolous, or trivial.

4. Think about whether the reading is capable of leading the listeners beyond their current understanding of life and love. Does it open to the possibility of learning more about love than you know now?

5. Does the reading express a timeless truth? Does it continue to seem fresh and wise over the ages?

Some Suggested Readings

"This Marriage"
by Jelaluddin Rumi, thirteenth-century poet

This marriage be wine with halvah,
honey dissolving in milk.
This marriage be the leaves and

fruit of a date tree.
This marriage be women

laughing together for days on end.
This marriage, a sign for us to study.

This marriage, beauty.
This marriage, a moon in a light blue sky.
This marriage, this silence fully
mixed with spirit.

Lao Tsu's *Tao Te Ching*

Practice nonaction. Work without doing. Taste the tasteless. Magnify the small. Increase the few. Reward bitterness with care. See simplicity in the complicated. Achieve greatness in little things. In the universe things are done as if they are easy. In the universe great acts are made up of small deeds. Easy promises are made for little trust. Taking things lightly result in great difficulty. And most of all remember that your love requires space in which to grow. This space must be safe enough to allow your heats to be revealed.

Native American Prayer

Be swift like the wind in loving each other.
Be brave like the sea in loving each other.
Be gentle like the breeze in loving each other.
Be patient like the sun who waits and watches
the four changes of the earth in loving each other.
Be wise like the roaring of the thunderclouds
and lightening in loving each other.
Be shining like the morning dawn in loving each other.
Be proud like the tree that stands without bending in
loving each other.

Be brilliant like the rainbow colors in loving each other.
Now, forever, forever, there will be no more loneliness.
Because your worlds are joined together with the world.
Forever. Forever.

From *The Prophet*
by Kahlil Gibran
On Marriage:

You were born together, and together you
shall be forever more.
You shall be together when the white wings of
death scatter your days.
Ah, you shall be together even in the silent
memory of God.
But let there be spaces in your togetherness,
and let the winds of heavens dance between you.
Love one another, but make not a bond of love.
let it rather be a moving sea between the
shores of your souls
Fill each other's cup but drink not from one cup.
Give one another of your bread, but eat not
from the same loaf.
Sing and dance together and be joyous,
but let each of you be alone.
Even as the strings of a lute are alone though
they quiver with the same music.
Give your hearts, but not into each other's keeping.
For only the hand of Life can contain your hearts
And stand together, yet not too near together:

For the pillars of the temple stand apart,
And the oak tree and the cypress grow not in each
other's shadow.

From verses by Walt Whitman

I do not offer the old smooth prizes, but offer rough
new prizes.
These are the days that must happen to you:
You shall not heap up what is called riches,
You shall scatter with lavish hands all that you earn or achieve.
However sweet the laid-up stores,
However convenient the dwellings,
You shall not remain there.
However sheltered the port,
And however calm the waters,
You shall not anchor there.
However welcome the hospitality that welcomes you.
You are permitted to receive it but a little while
Afoot and lighthearted, take to the open road,
Healthy, free, the world before you,
The long brown path before you, lading wherever
you choose.
Say only to one another:
Friend, I give you my hand!
I give you my love, more precious than money,
I give you myself before preaching or law:
Will you give me yourself?
Will you travel with me?
Shall we stick by each other as long as we live?

Winnie the Pooh
A. A. Milne

If you live to be a hundred,
I want to live to be a hundred minus one day,
so I never have to live without you.

The Song of Solomon, Chapter 2:10-13

My beloved spake, and said unto me, Rise up, my
love, my fair one, and come away.
For, lo, the winter is past, the rain is over and gone;
The flowers appear on the earth; the time of the
singing of birds is come, and the voice of the
turtle is heard in our land;
The fig tree putteth forth her green figs, and the
vines with the tender grape give a good smell.
Arise, my love, my fair one, and come away.

A Hundred Love Sonnets
by Pablo Neruda

When I die I want your hands on my eyes: I want
the white and wheat of your beloved hands to pass
their freshness over me once more. I want to feel the
softness that changed my destiny. I want you to live
while I wait for you asleep. I want your ears still to
hear the wind. I want to sniff the seas aroma that we
loved together; to continue to walk on the sand we
walk on. I want what I love to continue to live and

you whom I love and sang above everything else to continue to flourish full flowered: so that you can reach everything my Love directs you to so that my shadow can travel along in your hair so that everything can learn the reason for my song.

From *365 Tao, Daily Meditations*

It is difficult to go through life alone. We all need support and the sense of belonging that comes from working toward goals shared with another. For such a relationship to work, there must be basic compatibility of values, outlook, and purpose.

It is an inadequate cliché that husband and wife must be friends as well as lovers. Two mates can know loyalty found in no other type of relationship. Yet even in the face of such strength, the laws of nature remind us the need for moderation.

False attachments to another can become an addiction, a voluntary bondage detrimental to clear perception. We should not bind another to ourselves, should not define ourselves by our marriage or should not force another to stay with us. But if chance allows us to walk together, who is to challenge our choice of walking companions?

The beauty of marriage is like the fleeting
perfection of a snowflake.

A Hundred Love Sonnets
by Pablo Neruda

Two happy lovers make one bread, a single moon drop in the grass. Walking, they cast two shadows that flow together; waking, they leave one sun empty in their bed.

Of all the possible truths, they chose that day; they held it, not with ropes, but with an aroma. They did not shred the peace; they did not shatter words; their happiness is a transparent tower.

The air and wine accompany the lovers. The night delights them with its joyous petals. They have a right to all the carnations.

Two happy lovers, without an ending, with no death, they are born, they die, many times while they live; they have the eternal life of the Natural.

Paul L'Herrou

The hand which you each offer to the other is an extension of yourselves, just as is the warmth and love which you express to each other. Cherish the touch, for you are touching another life. Be sensitive to its pulse, and try to understand and respect its flow and rhythm, just as you do your own.

Shakespeare's Sonnet No. 116

Let me not to the marriage of true minds admit impediments. Love is not love which alters when it alteration finds, or bends with the remover to remove: Oh, no! It is on ever-fixed mark that looks on tempests and is never shaken; whose worth's unknown, although his height be taken. Love's not Time's foot, though rosy lips and cheeks. Within his bending sickle's compass come; Love alters not with his brief hours and weeks. But bears it out even to the edge of doom. If this be error and upon me proved. I never writ, nor no man ever loved.

The Prince's Choice
Thomas Reynolds Lamont

Sooner or later we begin to understand that love is more than verses on valentines and romance in the movies. We begin to know that love is here and now, real and true, the most important thing in our lives. For love is the creator of our favorite memories and the foundation of our fondest dreams. Love is a promise that is always kept, a fortune that can never be spent, a seed that can flourish in even the most unlikely of places. And this radiance that never fades, this mysterious and magical joy, is the greatest treasure of all—one known only by those who love.

Symbols Used in Weddings

Around 100 BCE, couples would traditionally eat small sweet cakes during the wedding service. Then, in the Middle Ages, food tossing became rice tossing. Nowadays, rice is out, and birdseed is in! There are many symbols to incorporate into your wedding service making it personalized and spiritual.

For example, the unity candle is lit usually by the bride and groom. For a twist, invite the parents to come forward and take part. In one wedding, everyone was given a candle at the beginning of the ceremony. During the lighting of the candle, two ushers went down on either side of the aisles and began lighting the candles of the guests seated on the outside of each row. Then, each person lit the candle of the person next to him or her, thus having everyone take part in this ritual. In another wedding, all the guests were seated at the tables during the ceremony. In the middle of each table, there was a candle inside a sconce. Two ushers went around to all the tables and lit the candles. Then they came to the front and lit the couple's candles; the couple, in turn, lit the main pillar candle.

On the following pages are different ceremonies within the ceremony that may be incorporated, along with words that may be used by the officiant. Of course, you already know about the familiar one—

the ring ceremony—but look at the variations for personalizing your own wedding ceremony.

Wine Ceremony

Couples may choose to share a goblet containing wine or water during their ceremony. There are many different types of goblets that may be purchased and later used during your marriage as symbols and reminders of your wedding day. When purchasing your goblet, you may want to take a special day off; and after your purchase, you may plan on having a picnic to celebrate.

During the ceremony the officiant may use the following words:

In this glass are the fruits of God, Mankind, and Mother Earth. The years of our lives are like a cup of wine that is poured out for the sake of labor, honor, and love.

Many days you will sit at the same table and eat and drink together. Many are the experiences you will share. As with a glass of wine, one of you may find it sweet, the other perhaps dry and somehow different. Let the drink you share today serve as a reminder that although you may perceive things very differently, being right is never more important than being happy. With this space that you give each other, always putting your commitment to love and honor one another first, your lives together will grow deeper, richer, and greatly satisfying, like a rare and fine wine.

You may ask a relative to come forward and pour the wine from a vessel into the goblet. Each takes a drink given by the other.

Water Ceremony

The officiant may use these words:

There is a saying in Eastern tradition that when you have love, even plain water is sweet. The clear water that you share today reflects the beauty and simplicity that is available to you both in remembering and devoting yourselves to the principal of love in your marriage. May it grow sweeter with each passing year.

Couple gives each other a drink from the same glass.

Flowers

Flowers are such a meaningful and beautiful part of the ceremony. Selecting a bridal bouquet of flowers for the couple's mothers should be done carefully.

But to make flowers a part of the ceremony in words as well as in what is seen is special. One groom always presented his bride with flowers during their courtship. When they became engaged, he strewed roses all over the house and placed the ring in the midst of a pile of petals that were on the fireplace. At the wedding, I spoke of this romantic gesture. I took petals from a basket, and as I spoke of this, I walked around the couple sprinkling the rose petals.

Flower Ceremony

Many couples wish to present their mothers a rose in honor of who they are and all that they have done.

If the theme of the wedding is, for example, sunflowers, couples may wish to present sunflowers instead. They also may wish to include grandparents as well.

In the presentation of the flower, the couple should go together to one mother at a time rather than separate and go to their own mother.

In Hindu weddings, couples wear with floral garlands that are placed over their necks during the beginning of the ceremony.

At the end of the ceremony, they remove them and present them to their mothers or both parents. The groom gives his garland to the bride's mother and vice versa.

Handfasting

Throughout history, couples have participated in a handfasting ceremony. A handfasting ceremony consists of choosing a family sash, a handmade cloth, or a store-bought ribbon. Whatever you select to tie around your hands, the fun is in the picking. I remember one couple who used their Scottish plaid pattern. Another couple bought a lovely ribbon with the word "Remembering" embossed on cream-colored silk. I feel the most important thing is to keep the sash narrow and fairly long in order for it to be loosely tied around the couple's hands. This sash can be used after you are married during one of your rituals.

Words that can be used during the ceremony are as follows:

> *In days gone by this ritual was considered a marriage contract by the joining of hands. And now together, the couple will place their hands facing inward toward each other and outward toward the world. The actual tying pattern is a symbol of infinity.*

> *The sash is tied loosely as they are bound to each other of their own free wills . . . a bond formed by love. A sign of love and faith, this ritual is the origin of the phrase "tying the knot."*

Family Ceremony

The family ceremony blesses the joined family and all its members. It can also be a time when second marriages with children can be honored. Children and stepchildren can step forward and receive a token of remembrance of the wedding. It can be a cross, a St. Christopher's medal, or a family medallion, which may be ordered from www.familymedallion.com. Special words can be said, and a blessing of the family and the articles can be administered.

Extended families can take all types of shapes and forms. I recently performed a lovely wedding where the groom was a firefighter, and this calling was very important to him. We honored his extended family—the firefighters—by calling their attention and reciting the Firefighters' Prayer.

Many couples want their pets to be included in the ceremony by either naming them or having them present. A dog can be a ring bearer. One bride owned many animals and worked with animals on a farm. We acknowledged all her pets by naming them and then honoring all of her extended animal family with a blessing of animals and saying the St. Francis prayer.

Blessing Stones

When a wedding is outside or near water, blessing or wishing stones may be gathered at the site or provided by the couple. Selecting the stones can be done together and made into a special time. After the ceremony, all guests follow the bride and groom's recessional to the water. Each guest takes a stone, makes a wish, and casts it in the water. The ripples from the water represent the love and good wishes not only for the couple but also for the entire world. I use the stone blessing at the site of rivers, ponds, and the ocean.

Ring Ceremony

The rings symbolize the love and bond between husband and wife. The wedding ring has been a traditional symbol of commitment and enduring love that, like a circle, is without beginning and without end.

The circle is also a reminder of what in Eastern traditions is called the wheel of life—which turns as we go through life, carrying us around and around through good times and difficult times, joy and sorrow, times of increase and times of decrease.

If we can position ourselves at the hub of the wheel, then as the wheel turns we remain centered and less affected by these vicissitudes of everyday circumstances.

Your choice to be married to one another can be a choice to step together into this center, to be a source of constancy for and with one another, through the ups and downs of life. The rings you exchange symbolize this choice and should be done with care.

Unity Candle

As I mentioned in the beginning, the lighting of the unity candle can be adapted in many ways. By providing all the guests with candles, so they may take part in the ceremony, is dramatic especially when it is an evening service.

The individual candles (tapers) that both the bride and groom hold represent each individually and the ties to family. The middle or pillar candle (unity candle) represents the marriage and the joining of both individuals and their families. The side tapers can be blown out after the unity candle is lit to represent the start of your new life together or they can remain burning to signify the blending of your unique family.

Some of the words that may be used by the officiant to bless this part of the ceremony are as follows:

> *Today you have pledged yourselves to a relationship of caring for one another in mutually fulfilling ways. May your togetherness always bring you joy and comfort and may your uniqueness continue to challenge you to live life with courage and creativity. And may the blessing of Light be with you always. Light without and*

light within. May the sun shine upon you and warm your heart until it glows like a great fire. So that others may feel the warmth of your love for one another and for the whole of creation. Amen.

Honoring the Cardinal Directions

Sometimes couples like to begin their ceremony by honoring the cardinal directions—north, south, east, and west, and also the center. Four candles are placed on the outside of the circle in the four directions, and someone from the wedding party is chosen to light the candles. As the officiant says the following words, the designated person slowly moves from candle to candle.

From the east I come to offer blessings.

For the powers of the wind, I wish you wisdom in hardship, laugher in joy, trust in each other. I offer blessings over all beginnings you ever choose together and the brightness of all dawning times. Yellow represents the East.

From the south I come to offer blessings.

For the powers of the fire, I wish you strength over grimness, light in darkness, pride in each other. I offer blessings over all things you are passionate in together and the warmth of flame in the joining of your souls. Under the glory of our sun, I offer blessings, in the name of all guardians. Red represents the South.

From the west I come to offer blessings.

For the powers of the sea, I wish you compassion in grief, patience in frustration, delights in each other. I offer blessings over all laughter you share together and the calm of the eternal waves under moonlight. Above the sparkle of the oceans, I offer blessings in the name of all lovers. Blue represents the West.

From the north I come to offer blessings.

For the powers of the mountain, I wish you fortitude in delay, beauty in stillness, support in each other. Offer blessings over all things lasting you hold together and the glow at the heart of an ember. Above the eternity of the rising earth, I offer blessings in the name of all heroes. Green represents the North.

And from within I come to offer blessings.

For the powers of those without, I wish you delight in life, diversity in unity, love always. I offer blessings over all companions traveled with together and true hearts to share unstintingly. In heartfelt love and delight, I offer blessings in the name of all friends.

Combining Rituals from the Christian and Jewish Traditions

Ringing Bells and Breaking the Glass

At the end of Christian ceremonies, we hear bells ringing; and in Jewish traditions, we hear the breaking of the glass. Among the many old interpretations of these two customs, one is that the loud noise of both the bells and the breaking of glass scare away evil spirits wishing harm to the newly married couple.

Breaking a glass summons the notion that sweetness can only exist alongside bitterness. Breaking the glass reminds us that although this wedding has provided joy, the world is still in turmoil and requires our care and love.

Glass breaking is not only a reminder of sorrow but also an expression of hope for a future free from all violence. The tradition of the breaking of the glass is a symbolic prayer and hope that the couple's love for one another will remain until the pieces of this glass come together again.

It is wise to wrap the glass or light bulb in a large napkin. There are many holders or boxes that can be bought to hold the shards of glass for remembrance.

Seven Hebrew Wedding Blessings

The following is included in Jewish weddings, but why not consider them in mixed marriages? As an officiant, it is wise to explain the custom as it is being done. The following explains the meanings of the seven Hebrew wedding blessings:

The first blessing is "Kiddush"—sanctification of God's name over wine.

The second and third blessings celebrating the theme of creation are the sequence that builds to the blessing of marriage.

The fourth blessing is a challenge to fulfill the potential for creativity, blessing, and peace.

The fifth blessing affirms that the bride and groom's marriage is made up of both passion and friendship.

The sixth blessing is for the bride and groom separately. Their relationship as beloved companions requires that each be able to stand alone even as they come together, bringing individual gifts to the marriage.

*The seventh blessing brings the bride and groom
to rejoice together, united in gladness.*

The Blessings

*Blessed art Thou, O Lord our God, King of the Universe,
who created the fruit of the vine, symbol of joy.*

*Blessed art Thou, O Lord our God, King of the Universe,
who has created all things to your glory.*

*Blessed art Thou, O Lord our God, King of the Universe,
Creator of man and woman.*

*Blessed are Thou, O Lord our God, King of the Universe,
who creates us to share with you in life's everlasting
renewal.*

*Blessed are Thou, O Lord our God, King of the Universe,
who causes Zion to rejoice at her children's return.*

*Blessed art Thou, O Lord our God, King of the Universe,
who causes bridegroom and bride to rejoice. May these
loving companions rejoice, as have your creatures since
the days of Creation.*

*Blessed are Thou, O Lord our God, King of the Universe,
who has created joy and gladness, bridegroom and bride,
mirth and exaltation, pleasure and delight, love,
brotherhood, peace, and fellowship.*

The Ketubah

Hebrew Marriage Contract

Since ancient times, the Ketubah or Hebrew marriage contract has been a long-standing tradition. First of all, this document and the meaning behind it express the bride and groom's promise and commitment to love and honor one another. It is also a work of art. It possesses a powerful and meaningful expression of how a couple wishes to live their life together. In each Ketubah, the artwork and words reflected are individual.

Couples use the words from the Ketubah within the context of their weddings. They could use them as part of their vows.

An Interfaith Ketubah can be purchased from the GOOD COMPANY located in Chicago, and these documents express the words suitable for couples of different religious traditions.

A special closed ceremony prior to the wedding service can be held where the immediate family is invited; the words are read, and the document can be signed. On the following page is an example of the words used in one document:

We pledge to each other to be loving friends and partners in marriage; to talk and listen, support, comfort, and strengthen each other's life's sorrows and joys.

We further promise to share hopes, thoughts,
and dreams as we build our lives together.
May we grow our lives ever intertwined, our love
bringing us closer.

We shall endeavor to establish a home that is compassionate to
all wherein the flow of the seasons and the passages of life, as
witnessed by our mutual traditions, are revered
and

honored. May our home be forever filled with peace,
happiness, and love.

Bringing Spirituality into Your Life Together After the "I Do's"

Goals and Values

The ceremony and honeymoon are over. *Whew!* Now let's talk about some goals and values for your relationship. Do your goals reflect your values? Do you know what is important to you?

Here are some questions that will stimulate your thoughts in deciding what values may be real for you. Don't be intimidated. Have fun. Here is a list of some core values: being self-reliant, capable, forgiving, tidy, loving, polite, daring, honest, truthful, responsible, open-minded, and the list goes on.

But let's look between the lines. Our values emerge in our choice of work, how we relate to people, how we spend our time, and how we think.

Plan to do some private work on answering these questions first, and then come together to see your similarities and differences.

A.

1. If you could do anything you wanted for one week, what would you do?

2. What three things do you want people to remember about you?

3. Finish this sentence: "Happiness is . . ."

4. What always makes you angry?

B. What is important to you in your personal relations and life experiences? Rate the following on a scale of 1 to 10 (1 being the lowest and 10 being the highest valued), and share with each other why each is important. Remember, you may not have the same results, but finding out the reasons behind the decisions is the important factor. Look at the sharing as fun and a new experience.

A chance to be creative.
Making a difference in the world.
Freedom to make your own decisions.
A beautiful home.
Optimal health.
Honesty with friends.
Peace in the world.
To be treated fairly.
Confidence in yourself.
Influence in your community.
A spiritual life.
A religious faith.
Orderliness in your affairs.
Wealth.
Others.

Journaling

The closer we are to being the directors in our own lives, the more we can share and become responsive to each other. This is what we can expect when we take the time to journal.

You will need some relaxed time and some sort of a notebook. It is important that neither of you try to influence what the other is doing, but rather wait until you are both finished to share your thoughts.

When you are journaling, it is best to just freely write down your thoughts with no self-judgment or criticism—just free-flowing form of ideas.

1. The first thing to do is to list all the major areas of your life. What do you want to bring into your life in the areas of love, home, work, play, health, finance, career, independence, travel, recreation, self-confidence building, personal growth, and relationships? Take your time and expound on your ideas, add new ones and take away those which do not serve you any longer.

2. Take a look at some of the following ideas and write about them.

   a. List what you do not want. List what you do want.

b. What dreams have not lived yet in your life?

c. What have you always wanted to do or be?

d. What would you do if you could do anything you wanted to do for one year?

e. How much money would you like to be making in a year? In five years?

Daydream a bit and see where your thoughts lead. Sometimes those long-hidden wants reveal themselves. Wishing is only a start. These are just some questions and thoughts you may want to tease yourself with. Expressing these desires to one another may be hard, or it may open up some wonderful new plans and new ideas. Go for it.

Frame Your Special Words

I did not include words from Paul's Letter to 1 Corinthians 13 in the "Readings" section of this book. I chose not to because so many couples are familiar with this reading. Yet even though it is popular, it is very beautiful. Instead I placed it in this section.

Many couples decide to frame one of their readings, their vows, or some other memorable and heartfelt words that may have been said during their wedding ceremony and hang it on the wall.

One couple I married not only framed their words but also recited them to each other every night just before they went to sleep. This reminder and constant expression of love kept their relationship spiritually complete.

Here are the words from Paul's letters, not necessarily for you to frame but as a reminder to either use them or find something more personal and suitable for your likes. Take your time to select something, and enjoy the process. And if you choose to read them to each other afterwards, then take the time and share the love that goes with it.

> *Love is patient and kind;*
> *Love is not jealous or boastful;*
> *it is not arrogant or rude.*

Love does not insist on its own way;
it is not irritable or resentful;
it does not rejoice at wrong,
but rejoices in the truth.
Love bears all things, believes all things,
hopes all things, and endures all things.
Love never gives up.
Love is eternal and never ends.

Let Your Love Bloom

Did you know the butterfly is "cellularly" wired for wings? When it enters the cocoon stage, wrapping itself up like a mummy, it actually breaks down and reforms again. It does not take the butterfly form from the original shape, but it actually transforms. It locates the cells for wings, and voila, it leaves the chrysalis and birth takes place.

I am not talking in a scientific way here, but let's face it; the metamorphosis of a butterfly is truly a remarkable concept. Let's equate the butterfly to your relationship. First, you were individuals having your own life and your own thoughts. You met each other and, in many cases, had to rethink some of your old values, your old ideas, and take up new ones. You had to reform yourselves and your ways. Then after you became married, you metamorphosed into the relationship which you are now a part.

Here is an idea to immortalize the butterfly concept in your lives. I know, you are busy with your new life. You are making plans for a home, maybe a baby, maybe a new business. I also know that it is good to create those time-outs together so that the foundation you are building together is strong and straight and true.

This idea can take time, but I encourage you to think about it or the one that follows. It is a project that you can do together, and it will bring spiritual growth to you individually and to your relationship. Every time you look at it, you will remind yourselves of your life together and your intentions.

Building a Butterfly Garden

Yes, I am suggesting you build a butterfly garden. Now I know some of you may not have a house or a condo yet, but this is a good project to hold over until you do. And whether you presently live in a house or a condo, a butterfly garden can be designed for different size gardens.

You start by looking up designs and history in different books and, of course, online. The hard part is digging up the soil, filling in with compost, and laying the bricks.

The fun part is picking appropriate flowers and planting them. In the book *Dreamscaping* by Ruth Rogers Clausen, some of the plants she included in her butterfly garden are butterfly bushes, sweet pepper bushes, asters, cornflowers, lavender, chives, coral bells, sedum, and fleabane. Check out this book also for a good layout design.

Select your location close to a porch or a deck, so you can view it when you sit down outside at the end of day.

Remembering and reminding yourselves of the days you spent designing this special dedication to your life together is the spiritual quality of this project, because it is not only for you but also for the enhancement of the environment.

> *Flowers are the beautiful hieroglyphics of*
> *nature with which she indicated how much she loves us.*
> —Johann von Goethe

Planting a Tree

One couple I married a few years ago decided to donate and plant a tree in the park where their ceremony took place. Each year they come back to the spot and revisit the growing symbol of their love. They take pictures, they have a picnic, and then as time passes, they bring their children.

Sometimes they bring their wedding album and provide enough time to look through it and recall the moments that meant so much to each other.

If your location for your wedding accepts this idea, you may want to build this into your ceremony and into your future spiritual times together. Pictures, picnics, and being together in the environment are the perfect way to celebrate and honor a special time.

Advice from a Tree

Stand tall and proud.
Sink your roots into the earth.
Be content with your natural beauty.
Go out on a limb.
Drink plenty of water.
Remember your roots.
Enjoy the view now.

(Copied from a poster printed
by Cottonwood Press)

Memory Albums

Your wedding was well documented by professional photographers and videographers, but what happens to those special times after the wedding? Maybe you stuff photos in a box. Maybe you even organize albums according to events and times, but more often than not, there may not be any rhyme or reason to your photo presentations.

But today, scrapbooks and memory albums are in big demand, and making them is an art. One company called Creative Memories has a fist load of consultants who specialize in providing workshops and materials to help people put together professional-looking albums.

One couple took it one step further. Periodically they take out their current photos and spread them out on a table. They pick the ones they want to place in the album and mount their selections. As they are placing them in the album, they also spend time on documenting their feelings, reactions, and memories about the incidences reflected in the photos by writing their findings next to each photo. As Amy Abel, album consultant, says, "The photos are one part of the remembrance, but equally important are the stories behind them."

What happens then is that couples find they remember things that the other partner did not recall. They share their remembrances, and this brings laughter and a new outlook on their relationship.

Try this idea and see a deeper closeness emerge.

Family Meetings

A couple who married a number of years ago and who now have two children not yet teenagers decided to hold family meetings once a week. They schedule them for the same time each week, and attendance is mandatory. The topics they discuss cover information about what they are doing, what they are thinking, and what they are feeling. However, the one main rule is that this is not an opportunity for them to complain about themselves or another person in the family. It is not a "venting" opportunity.

You may want to hold family meetings before you have children or else build them into your life when your children seem to be in the appropriate age. It is especially good to set the right feeling in the room you select for your meeting. Remember bringing in fragrances, maybe incense—candles are special. Sitting in circle gives everyone the feeling that all people are equals and each have an equal opportunity to share.

Happiness and Inner Peace

Happiness does not depend so much
on circumstances as on one's inner self.
—Lady Randolph Churchill

It was important for me to end this book with some selected words or ideas that I felt were poignant and could help guide you through your life together.

There are all sorts of resources and tips on how to find inner peace and how to bring happiness into your life.

I carefully searched and finally decided to include the titles of the chapters from Dr. Wayne Dyer's book, *Ten Secrets for Success and Inner Peace.*

A good project to do together might be to get the book and to use each chapter for reading and for discussion.

Along with other books, I use this particular one during my meditation times and have found it inspiring and useful. I encourage you do as well.

Key ideas in Dr. Dyer's book:

1. Have a mind that is open to everything and attached to nothing.

2. Don't die with your music still in you.

3. You can't give away what you don't have.

4. Embrace silence.

5. Give up your personal history.

6. You can't solve a problem with the same mind that created it.

7. There are no justified resentments.

8. Treat yourself as if you already are what you'd like to be.

9. Treasure your divinity.

10. Wisdom is avoiding all thoughts that weaken you.

A Partial List of Recommended Books

Interfaith Wedding Ceremonies—Guidance for a Jew and a Christian who plan to get married. Selected and with an introduction by Joan C. Hawxhurst. Published by Dovetail Publishing, Kalamazoo, Michigan.

Inviting God to Your Wedding—Martha Williamson. Published by Harmony Books, NY.

Life Prayers—Elizabeth Roberts and Elias Amidon. Published by HarperSanFrancisco.

Weddings by Design—Richard Leviton. Published by HarperSanFrancisco.

Wedding Vows—Michael MacFarlane. Published by Sterling Publishing Co, Inc., NY.

Sacred Threshold—Getrud Mueller Nelson and Christopher Witt. Published by Doubleday.

The Everything Wedding Vows Book—Janet Anastasio and Michelle Bevilacqua. Published by Adams Media Corporation, Massachusetts.

The Complete Idiot's Guide to Creative Weddings—Antonia van der Meer. Published by Alpha Books.

The Women's Book of Healing Herbs—Secrets from 90 Top Herbal Healers. Sari Harrar and Sara Altshul O' Donnell. Published by Rodale Press, PA.

Taking Time for Tea—Diana Rosen. Published by Storey Books, Vermont.

The Directory of Essential Oils—Wanda Sellar. Published by C. W. Daniel Company Limited, Essex, England.

Perfumes, Scented Gifts and Other Fragrances—Kelly Reno. Published by Prima Publishing, Roseville, CA.

Candles, Bubble Baths and Other Romantic Indulgences—Kelly Reno. Published by Prima Publishing, Roseville, CA.

The Essence of Incense—Diana Rosen. Published by Storey Books, Vermont.

The Book of Green Tea—Diana Rosen. Published by Storey Books, Vermont.

Peace be to you

and

most of all,

enjoy life together

and

have fun.

*This is your time to
enjoy these moments. It may
be rushed and you may have to make decisions that
become overwhelming, but take the time-out to breathe.
Remember, when you pick your
minister to handle the sacred part of your day, be sure to
take your time and base your selection on the fact that
you must be comfortable with that person.
I extend my best wishes to all so that you may enjoy your
special times together and to find unique ways to
celebrate your life together.*

Charlann Walker
Interfaith Minister
call me:
401 463-8796
email me:
revcharlann@yahoo.com
see my web page:
interfaithweddingministry.com

Let your love flow outward through the universe,
To its height, its depth, its broad extent,
A limitless love, without hatred or enmity.
Then as you stand or walk,
Sit or lie down,
As long as you are awake,
Strive for this with a one-pointed mind;
Your life will bring heaven to earth.

Suttra Nippatsu
Buddha's Discourse on Good Will

Endorsements

"Developing a Spiritual Partnership" meets deep needs. It meets and satisfies the needs of the marital couple, the Officiant, and humanity in general. It is a treasure trove of inspiration, education, and information, helping us to live, to breathe, to commune, and to unite on a profound level! Thank you Charlann Walker for your vision." Rev. Dr. Rainbow Johnson, International Minister of, The Church Without Walls and The Family Without Boundaries.

"Charlann Walker gets directly to the point in each section, making it easy and fast to understand. Her tips/advice/suggestions for remaining close before, during and after the "I do's" are sound pieces of information. Her personal input on what works for her is really helpful and makes everything attainable. This is a must book for couples who desire to bring spirituality into their lives making their relationship more sustainable and stronger." Nora Haynes, Publicist, GQ Magazine.

"Rev. Walker's book is clear, readable and invaluable for those wishing to learn many valuable lessons through the experience of others. Highly recommended." Barnett C. Helzberg Jr. author, *What I Learned Before I Sold to Warren Buffett*

"This great little guidebook, with its easy-to-implement suggestions, is not only useful for those planning their actual wedding ceremonies, but for any couple wanting a deep, loving and committed relationship. Try some of them and see for yourself!"
Judy Marcellot, The Peace Gardens at 7 Arrows (site of lots of interesting weddings over the years—conventional and not-so!)

"*Developing a Spiritual Partnership* is great! There are some super ideas. I (already being married) especially enjoyed the before and after the wedding parts. I loved the part about meditating together and mapping. I would like to map on smaller paper at different parts in our lives and put it all in a scrapbook."
Eileen Harris, yoga instructor

BVG